I0214254

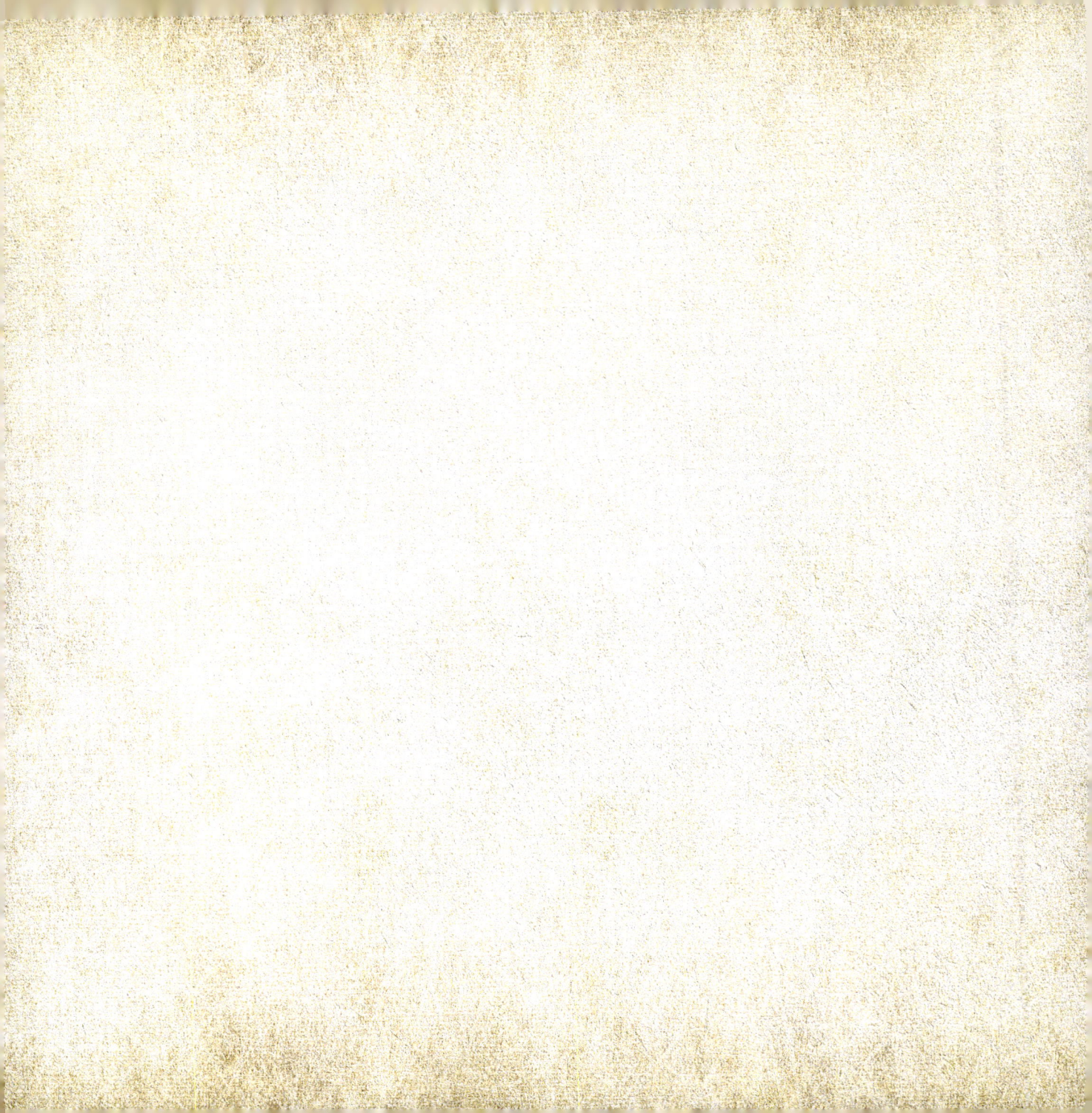

WILDERNESS
SPEAKS

Wild Soul Press

Boulder, Colorado

Copyright 2020 by Scott Stillman

The moral right of Scott Stillman to be identified as the author of this work has been asserted by him in accordance with the Copyright, Designs, and Patents Act of 1988. All rights reserved. Published in the United States by Wild Soul Press. No part of this book may be reproduced in any form or by any electronic means, without permission in writing from the publisher, except by a reviewer who may quote brief passages for a review.

Design and Layout: Victoria Wolf, Wolf Design and Marketing

Photographs by Scott Stillman

Library of Congress Cataloging-in-Publication Data
Stillman, Scott
Wilderness Speaks / Scott Stillman
LCCN 2020910378
ISBN: 978-1-7323522-4-7

WILDERNESS SPEAKS

SCOTT STILLMAN

WORDS AND PHOTOGRAPHY FROM
WILDERNESS, THE GATEWAY TO THE SOUL

WILD
SOUL
PRESS

True **magic** does exist,

Grand Staircase-Escalante National Monument, Utah

it just remains hidden,

Maroon Bells-Snowmass Wilderness, Colorado

not in the far reaches of our imagination,
but right here on Earth.

Eagle Cap Wilderness, Oregon

Tucked into deep valleys, rugged mountain ranges, and the **far reaches of this planet.**

Weminuche Wilderness, CO

Revealing itself only to those who are willing to
make the journey.

Death Hollow, Utah

Come on in, see for yourself.

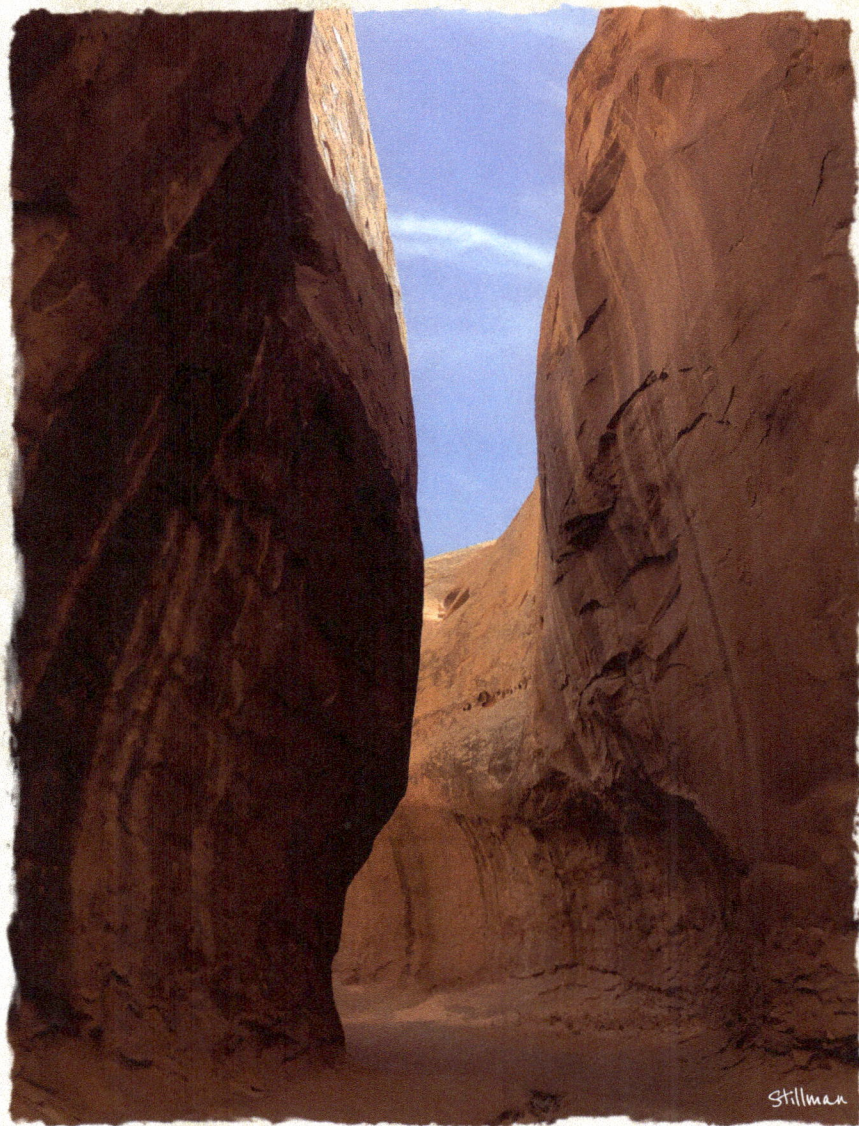

Glen Canyon National Recreation Area, Utah

17

Take a walk out onto these rocks and the story unfolds in high-definition color and startling clarity.

It's a walk through time.

Glen Canyon National Recreation Area, Utah

We all have a story to tell.

Here it is laid out like an open book.

Dirty Devil Wilderness, Utah

Around every corner we flip another page in
Earth's life sized history book.

Bears Ears National Monument, Utah

Bears Ears National Monument, Utah

Bears Ears National Monument, Utah

Everything has its story—some are hundreds of years old, others just minutes.
It's the greatest story ever told.

Humboldt Redwood State Park, California

Bears Ears National Monument, Utah

Bears Ears National Monument, Utah

They all seem to be saying the same thing:

"I WAS HERE."

Bears Ears National Monument, Utah

To hike quickly would be like racing through an art gallery.
Better to wander,
stroll, creep our way through.

Grand Staircase-Escalante National Monument, Utah

Dark Canyon Wilderness, Utah

Lee Metcalf Wilderness, Montana

This is a museum.
We are part of the exhibit,

Capital Reef National Park, Utah

leaving our footprints in the sand.

Oregon Coast Trail, Oregon

Art without the artist. Painting without the painter. The work of God.

Oregon Coast Trail, Oregon

Bridgeport, California

Mayflower Gulch, Colorado

Only when order and chaos reach perfect equilibrium can such **brilliance** occur.

Grand Staircase-Escalante National Monument, Utah

Lake Powell, Utah

Hanksville, Utah

There is primal wisdom deep within the fissures of the Earth. It's all right here. Ready for anyone who wishes to learn.

Grand Staircase-Escalante National Monument, Utah

Black Ridge Canyons Wilderness, Colorado

Black Ridge Canyons Wilderness, Colorado

It lies within all this silence and stillness.

A wisdom so profound that it transcends words.

An understanding so pure it cannot be explained, cannot be taught, nor grasped by the human mind.

Only felt. Experienced firsthand.

Pettit Lake, Idaho

Tucson, Arizona

Tucson, Arizona

In Wilderness, the sermon is delivered by no man, but rather by the rocks themselves, the air you breathe, the plants, the clouds, and the sky above.

North Cascades, Washington

There is wisdom in anarchy, precision in chaos. Everything here is in its perfect place, yet precisely out of order.

Tucson, Arizona

To truly understand a place like this, **we must lay our thinking minds aside** and breathe in the magic. Surrender to the mystery.

San Rafael Wilderness, Utah

Stop talking, stop thinking,
start listening.

Death Valley, Nevada

Flowers mastering the art of being flowers.

Stillman

Shooting Stars

Common Beargrass

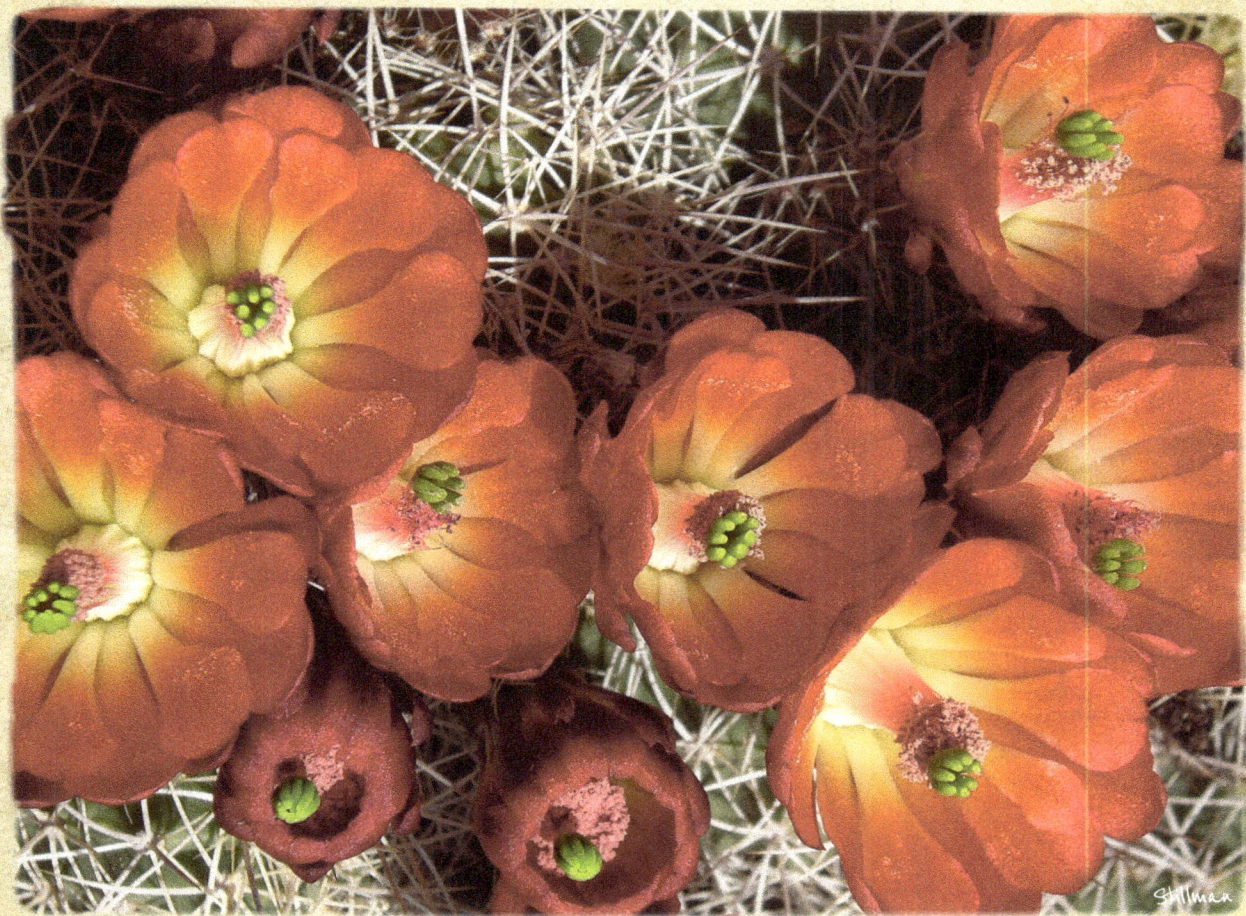

Scarlet Hedgehog Cactus

Ravens mastering the art of being ravens.

Natural Bridges National Monument, Utah

The land opens completely, revealing her most intimate secrets, her most sacred beauty.

Death Valley, Nevada

Death Valley, Nevada

Organ Pipe Cactus National Monument, Arizona

What is beauty?

Some say it lies within the observer.

Where we witness a canyon of pristine beauty,

others may see a desert wasteland,

inhospitable, uninhabitable, intolerable,

unprofitable.

Glen Canyon National Recreation Area, Utah

Beauty is a choice.

Day by day, moment by moment, we choose love or hate, life or death, light or darkness. The seeds for both are contained within all things.

It depends on what we focus on.

Big Sur, California

Tucson, Arizona

Bears Ears National Monument, Utah

Wilderness is the place to understand
the universe.

Eagle Cap Wilderness, Oregon

There is so much beauty, and
only so much time.

Seal Rock Beach, Oregon

When we surrender to the present moment,
accepting it for all its beauty and amazement,
the universe guides us to all
the right places.

Eagle Cap Wilderness, Oregon

Big South Fork National River and Recreation Area, Tennessee

Mount Washington Wilderness, Oregon

No matter how low you can get,
how much society lets you down,
you can always come back here.

Moab, Utah

You can always go home.

Maroon Bells-Snowmass Wilderness, Colorado

Wilderness calls, heaven waits, for those simply willing to GO.

Durango, Colorado

Even if we never come,

she exists the same.

Gothic, Colorado

Sometimes that is enough, just knowing
she is here.

Sierra Nevada Mountains, California

About the Author

Scott Stillman was born in Fairfield, Ohio, then moved to Boulder, Colorado in 2003. Backpacking extensively through the mountains and deserts of the American West, he records his journeys with pen and notebook—and occasionally camera and lens— writing primarily about our spiritual connection to nature.

Scott is bestselling author of *Wilderness, The Gateway to the Soul*, and the highly acclaimed follow-up, *Nature's Silent Message*.

As our culture continues to remove itself from the natural world, Scott's books provide refreshing insight that there's life outside the regiment—hope beyond the pavement.

He and his wife, Valerie, have lived in a truck camper and worked a slew of unconventional jobs to fund their travels and stay on the wilderness path.

You can find his blog and online home at:

scottstillmanblog.com

facebook.com/scottstillmanblog

If the mood strikes, send him an email at:

scottstillmanauthor@gmail.com

Enjoy this Book?
Write a Review!

If you've enjoyed my book, the best compliment you can give is writing a review. As a self-published indie author, I don't have the advertising power of a major publishing firm. But you can make a big difference.

Honest reviews help other readers find me. It only takes five minutes and the review can be as short as you like.

If you'd like to leave a review on Amazon.com, search for my title, click on **CUSTOMER REVIEWS**, then click **WRITE A CUSTOMER REVIEW**. Simple as that.

Thank you very much.

Dirt-Worshipping
Tree-Huggers Unite!

If you are interested in solo backpacking, or following along on my upcoming adventures via my blog, I'd love to connect with you!

Sign up for my mailing list and you'll gain access to:

- My ongoing travel essays.

- Exclusive photographs of wilderness areas from this book.

- Backpacking recipes, gear checklists, tips for finding your own Gateway to the Soul, and more.

You can sign up for my mailing list at
www.scottstillmanblog.com.

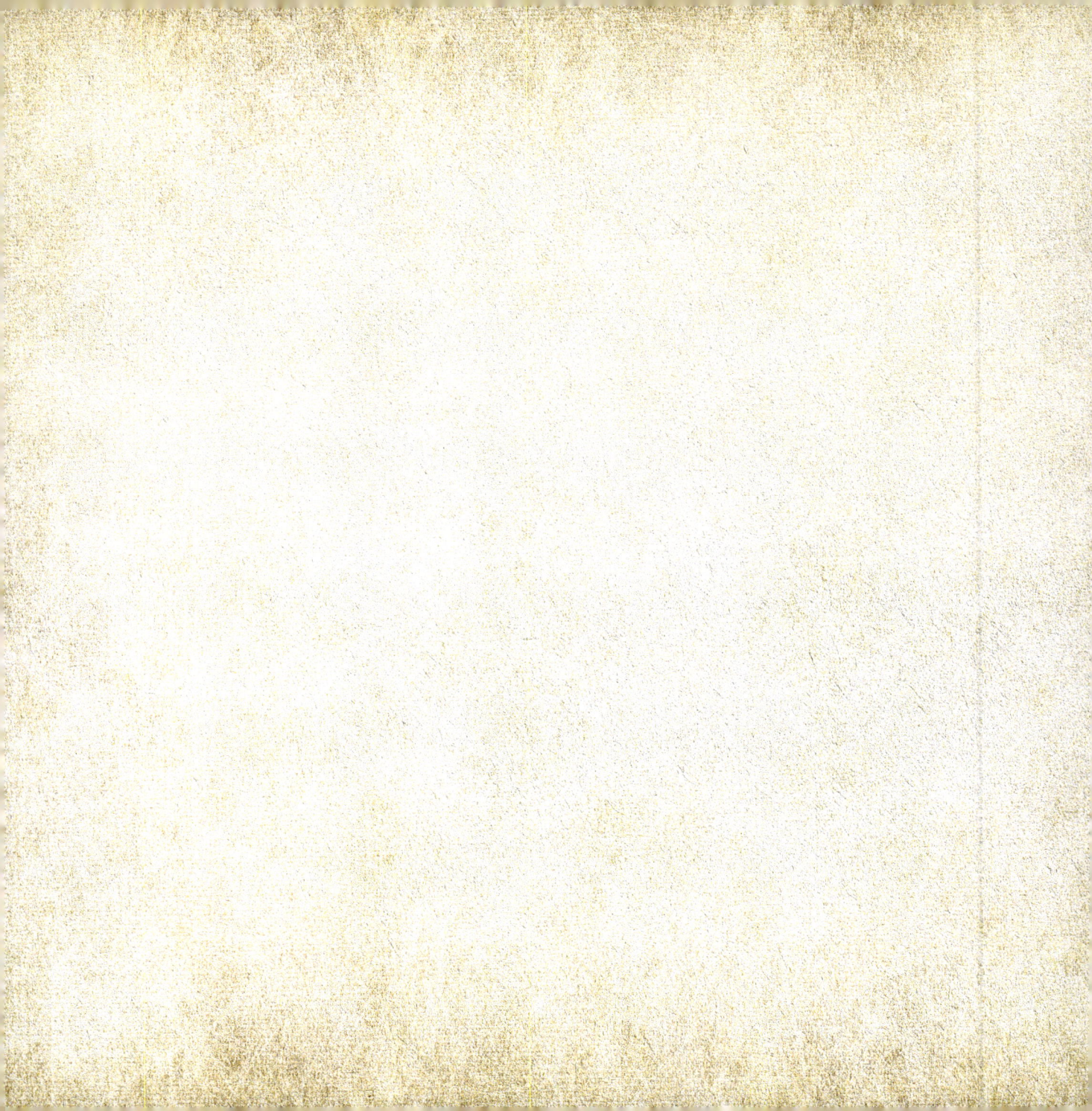

SAVE WILD UTAH!

SOUTHERN UTAH WILDERNESS ALLIANCE (SUWA)

SUWA is the only non-partisan, non-profit organization working full time to defend Utah's Redrock Wilderness from oil and gas development, unnecessary road construction, rampant off-road vehicle use, and other threats to Utah's wilderness-quality lands. Their power comes from people like you from across the nation who want to protect this irreplaceable heritage for all Americans.

If you'd like to get involved, please find them at www.suwa.org

SUWA

SOUTHERN UTAH WILDERNESS ALLIANCE

Index of Photographs

Bears Ears National Monument, Utah p. 23, 24, 25, 28, 29, 31, 79

Big South Fork National River and Recreation Area, Tennessee p. 86

Big Sur, California p. 77

Black Ridge Canyons Wilderness, Colorado p. 50, 51

Bridgeport, California p. 42

Capital Reef National Park, Utah p. 37

Common Beargrass p. 66

Dark Canyon Wilderness, Utah p. 34

Death Hollow, Utah p. 15

Death Valley, Nevada p. 63, 71, 72

Dirty Devil Wilderness, Utah p. 21

Durango, Colorado p. 93

Eagle Cap Wilderness, Oregon p. 11, 81, 85

Glen Canyon National Recreation Area, Utah p. 17, 19, 75

Gothic, Colorado p. 95

Grand Staircase-Escalante National Monument, Utah p. 7, 33, 45, 49

Hanksville, Utah p. 47

Humboldt Redwood State Park, California p. 27

Lake Powell, Utah p. 46

Lee Metcalf Wilderness, Montana p. 35

Maroon Bells-Snowmass Wilderness, Colorado p. 9, 91

Mayflower Gulch, Colorado p.43

Moab, Utah p. 89

Mount Washington Wilderness, Oregon p. 87

Natural Bridges National Monument, Utah p. 69

North Cascades, Washington p. 57

Oregon Coast Trail, Oregon p. 39, 41

Organ Pipe Cactus National Monument, Arizona p. 73

Pettit Lake, Idaho p. 53

San Rafael Wilderness, Utah p.61

Scarlet Hedgehog Cactus p. 67

Seal Rock Beach, Oregon p. 83

Shooting Stars p. 65

Sierra Nevada Mountains, California p. 97

Tucson, Arizona p. 54, 55, 59, 78

Weminuche Wilderness, Colorado p. 13

www.ingramcontent.com/pod-product-compliance
Lightning Source LLC
Chambersburg PA
CBHW060751150426
42811CB00058B/1370

9 781732 352247